LET'S GO TEAM:
Cheer, Dance, March

Competitive Cheerleading

Techniques of Dance for Cheerleading

History of Cheerleading

Techniques of Cheerleading

Chants, Cheers, and Jumps

Going to College

Dance Teams

Color Guard Competition

Techniques of Color Guard

Marching Band Competition

Techniques of Marching Bands

Cheerleading Stars

LET'S GO TEAM:
Cheer, Dance, March

Techniques of
COLOR GUARD

Karyn Sloan

Mason Crest Publishers
Philadelphia

Mason Crest Publishers, Inc.
370 Reed Road
Broomall, PA 19008
(866) MCP-BOOK (toll free)
www.masoncrest.com

2 3 4 5 6 7 8 9 10

Library of Congress Cataloging-in-Publication Data

Sloan, Karyn.
  Techniques of color guard / Karyn Sloan.
     p. cm. — (Let's go team — cheer, dance, march)
Includes index.
Summary: Describes the history and techniques of color guards, including
music, choreography, flag twirling, rifle twirling, teamwork and pageantry.
  ISBN 1-59084-536-6
1. Marching drills — Juvenile literature. 2. Color guards — Juvenile literature.
[1. Marching drills. 2. Color guards.] I. Title. II. Series.
  GV1797 .S56 2003
  791 — dc21
                    2002015956

Produced by
Choptank Syndicate and Chestnut Productions
226 South Washington Street
Easton, Maryland 21601

Project Editors Norman Macht and Mary Hull
Design Lisa Hochstein
Picture Research Mary Hull

Printed and bound in the Hashemite Kingdom of Jordan

OPPOSITE TITLE PAGE
*Color guard is known as "the sport of the arts" because it
combines precision movement with music, color, and artistic
choreography.*

Table of Contents

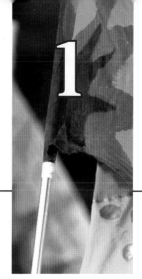

The Sport of the Arts

They suddenly turned off all the lights in the Indianapolis RCA Dome, which left the field lit only by the red "Exit" signs. It was the eerie cue given to the instructors to send their guards toward the field. Each marching band that had competed in the Bands of America Finals was waiting in full retreat on the field while their guards were above, hiding in the hallways behind the stands.

Moments after the audience's eyes adjusted to the dim light, they saw hundreds of guard members streaming down the aisles of the stands opposite them, running in single file to join their bands. White fireworks rained

The Purdue University Golden Silks add a splash of the school's black and gold colors during a halftime show. The Golden Silks perform with the marching band at home football games, selected away games, and campus and community events.

down from the dome's ceiling, lighting the field while the anxious guard members assembled in the front, striking their poses.

Giant screens on both sidelines dropped down and immediately began to display images that had been captured earlier that evening of the bands while they had performed. As each band's candid pictures scrolled by, cheers went up from the 10,000 people in the audience. Adrenaline pumping, the color guards waited for the lights to return so they could see who would receive the award for the Outstanding Color Guard.

This happens every year at the Bands of America Grand National Competition, and it's just one of the many amazing events a color guard can participate in. There is also Winter Guard International (WGI), an organization that is focused solely on indoor color guard. Some of the color guards that compete at these events practice year-round to perfect their shows. Drum Corps International (DCI) is another group that offers opportunities for competitive color guards and marching bands. At the college level, color guards perform at major Bowl Games, and are seen by millions of people on national television.

Color guard is known as the "sport of the arts" because it requires concentration, technique, rhythm, and grace. Color guards use flags and weapons, such as rifles and sabers. (The rifles and sabers are used as props and are not functional). Colorful costumes, intricate flag work, and complicated dance moves all complement the music.

Color guard is believed to have evolved from military color guards that presented their company's "colors" or

Color guards use many different types of flags in their performances. Weights are placed in the flagpoles to help the flags rotate properly when tossed.

flags. Eventually, military color guards presented flags during football games. During the 1920s, participants began to hold flags of different nations during halftime shows, and they moved in formations with the band. After that, different kinds of colored flags were incorporated to entertain the audience, dance moves were added, and color guard was born.

COLOR GUARD EQUIPMENT

Basic flagpoles are usually between five and six feet long and one and a quarter inches in diameter. Poles may be made of aluminum, PVC piping, plastic, or fiberglass. Poles for swing flags are much shorter in length. A swing flag usually is only a few inches longer than the silk that is attached to the pole, leaving enough room to be held without touching the silk. A T-pole is two poles connected together to form a "T." A long, rectangular silk is attached to the top of the "T," making this flag excellent for creating large circles. Chain flags, where a length of

COLOR AND WINTER GUARD

What is a color guard?
Color guard is the expression of music through the medium of movement. Basically a group of people perform a routine with equipment or dance to music. The most common form is the people you see dancing or spinning flags with a marching band during a halftime show.

What is a winter guard?
A winter guard is a color guard that performs during the winter months (usually the second semester of the school year) to taped music, although some are known to use live music.

Why join a guard?
Color guard is a lot like football—you don't truly understand it until you've participated. However, you can learn to appreciate it just by being a spectator. It can be addicting, beautiful, frustrating, and wonderful all in one instance. Just like any other sport, it takes practice to make it work, but just getting there is half the fun.

Performance rifles are usually white or black, and they can be used with or without straps. Because straps make a sound when the rifle is spun, they let guard members hear whether everyone is spinning in unison.

chain is threaded through a silk, can be collapsed into the hands, then suddenly revealed as if from nowhere. There are also wongas, short swing flags that bend with the drag of the silk; butterfly flags, which are two poles connected by a half-circle of silk; swivel poles, which are designed to prevent the silk from getting tangled; and many other variations.

At the end of each pole there are rubber or plastic stoppers that cap off the pole. A more advanced guard will have weights inside their poles. The type of weight depends on the silk and the length of the pole. The most common weight is two bolts, one long and one short. The long one is put in the top of the pole (the silk end) and the short in the bottom. The bolts should be taped to prevent them from flying out in case a stopper comes off. The silk has drag and the bare pole side does not. When tossing, these weights help the flag rotate properly. Surprisingly, the more weight you add, the higher your toss will go.

Let's Go Team Technique Tip: Cover your bolts with plastic or vinyl electrical tape. This will keep the bolt from chewing up the end of the pole and the bottom of the bolt from clanking against the pole.

Rifles are constructed of wood with a metal bolt attached to the top, where the ammunition would go if it were actually a gun. Rifle lengths vary, but are usually somewhere between 32 and 40 inches. Practice rifles are wrapped with thick strapping tape. Two protective pads are placed on the ends to prevent the rifle from splitting or cracking if it is dropped. A performance rifle's bolt is shiny silver; the rifle is either white or black. Some rifles have straps made of nylon web or leather, attached on the underside of the rifle. When the rifle is spun the strap slaps against the neck of the rifle, letting a guard hear if everyone is spinning in tempo.

Sabers (also spelled "sabres") are long swords that have a handle at the end. The blades are usually white plastic or metal. Like rifles, they come in many different lengths between 32 and 40 inches. Sabers are a more complicated weapon than rifles and are difficult to see from far away. They are not as common as rifles among color guards.

The blade of the saber is dulled or sheathed with tape; color guard members who handle sabers may also wear gloves for added protection.

Most color guards use additional equipment in their shows such as action ribbons, batons, or scarves. Depending on a show, color guards might find that these props help accent their music better than a flag could. However, if you see color guard members out on the field with pom pons, they might be a drill team. A drill team

Sometimes guard members use extra props like streamers or ribbons, as shown by a member of the Joliet Kingsmen Drum Corps Color Guard from Joliet, Illinois.

usually just dances and uses the poms, whereas color guards rely more on the flags for expression.

This book covers some of the more basic flag positions and works into more advanced moves that are common in color guard today. Following the technique chapters, choreography is broken down into easy steps along with information to help understand movement and drill, which serve to complement any routine. The final chapter discusses the opportunities available to those interested in joining a color guard and what steps to take to get there. This book gives you virtually everything you need to get a good start in color guard.

Beginning Technique

This book focuses on color guard technique for North America, but it is important to note that terms are not always standard from region to region. Depending on where an instructor trained, the terms they use might differ from the ones listed here.

POSITIONS

When doing any sort of flag work, it's important to pay attention to other parts of your body besides your arms. Are your feet together or apart? Some people like to stand with their feet planted a shoulder's width apart for stability. Others think standing with the heels together is more

It takes practice to master the drop spin, which should be done at waist level. It's also important to keep your head up and your eyes looking straight ahead.

attractive. Either of these stances is fine, but if you decide to stand with your feet together, try placing your feet in what ballet dancers call **third position.** To do this, turn your left foot out slightly and place the heel of your right beside the arch of your left. Your feet should form a nice "T." This stance tends to cause people to stand up straight and present their chest up, a position color guards are always striving to maintain.

Now let's talk about the most fundamental position: **right shoulder.** Practically every move or spin begins with right shoulder, so it is very important to master this position. Without this position, it would be like trying to read without vowels. Right shoulder is given its name because the right shoulder is up; your right hand is on top. So at left shoulder, your left hand is on top. No matter how tall or short you are, this position is the same for everyone, so make sure you follow the description closely.

Grasp the pole where the silk stops with your right hand, thumb on top. Then grasp with your left hand down at the bottom of the pole, so that your left hand covers the stopper. Your left hand should be the same as your right—thumb on top—and directly in front of your bellybutton. Make sure your pole runs straight up and down. A good way to check this is to make sure you are standing up straight and the pole is between your eyes. Present your chest up and raise your eyes a bit above the horizon. This is a great habit to get into because it makes you look confident.

Practice right shoulder until you are comfortable with it. Check with a friend to make sure your pole is straight

The Purdue University Golden Silks demonstrate the right shoulder position. Right shoulder is the most basic position in color guard and most spins and moves start from this position.

and you're not hunched over, burying the stopper in your stomach. Use a mirror if you have room or try the position without the flag. Keep your elbows a little distance from your body; they should bend comfortably to allow the position. It's important to know this position since most movement stems from it.

Another common flag position is the **slam.** The name "slam" comes from the way you achieve this angle; it looks like the flag is at right shoulder, but the top stopper

In the slam position, your left hand will be just above your left shoulder and your right hand will be near your hip, with the silk pointed down and the flag cutting across your body at a 45-degree angle.

is slammed down toward the ground. To duplicate this position, go to right shoulder, then drop the tip of the flag down toward the floor, allowing your left hand to go up. Don't actually rest the tip on the floor; make sure there's a few inches between the stopper and the ground. Your hands should be the same as they were at right shoulder, but now your thumbs should be pointing toward the ground. Your left hand should be just a few inches above your left shoulder, and your right hand a few inches from your right hip. The flag pole should cut across your body at a 45-degree angle, the silk part down.

Make sure your right palm is facing up toward the sky, and your left palm is facing down. Both of your elbows should be bent comfortably and you should be standing straight and tall. Check your angle repeatedly, making sure it is a nice diagonal. If someone drew a large square in front of you, your flag would run from the top left

TYPES OF FLAGS

The most basic equipment in color guard is a flag. Here are a few of the most common types:

Swing flag. The silk is attached to an approximately three-foot pole, leaving just enough room for one hand to grip it at the bottom.

Chain flag. The silk is threaded with a heavy metal chain, allowing the user to bunch the flag up and wrap it around the body.

Regular flag. A basic flag has stoppers at either end of the pole, which can vary in length, with 5' to 5' 5" being common.

Half-and-half flags. With this type of flag about three feet of the pole is metal, but the rest of it is made from PVC piping. PVC piping is more difficult to twirl, but it also offers more drag. The advantage of a half and half pole is the metal part can be twirled and tossed, and the PVC part gives drag.

Butterfly flags. These are flags on which the silk is attached at both ends, with room to grip the pole in the middle. It generates the effect of spinning two flags at once.

corner to the bottom right, splitting the square into two equal triangles.

Now that you understand right shoulder and slams, let's move on to another position: **flat.** Flat is a relatively easy position—the flag just lies flat in your hands. The flag should be parallel to the ground, regardless of what flat you're at. Perhaps you want the flat at your waist, in line with your belt. If you want to be flat at your eyes, the pole should be directly in front of your eyes, parallel to the ground, one hand at the bottom of the silk and the other at the bottom stopper. When you are at a flat, your arms should be an equal distance from your body. If you are flat at your waist, the center of the bare pole should be right in front of your belt buckle.

The **attention**—or "ready"—position is the position that color guards come to before starting a routine, or during marching drills and parades. Like right shoulder, your right hand grabs the pole at the bottom of the silk, but instead of being up above your head, your right hand is out in front of your waist. Your left grabs halfway in the silk, and your forearm is parallel to the ground. Think about resting your left arm on an invisible table. At first it may feel a bit uncomfortable or your arm may get tired. Practice will strengthen your arm and help keep your elbow from slowly dipping down. This is a great position to practice in front of a mirror or with a friend. Make sure you're standing tall, the pole is straight, and your left arm is out. Don't let that left elbow drop.

From the attention position, you can easily go up to right shoulder. Just let go with your left hand and bring

Color guard members assume the attention or "ready" position before beginning a routine.

your right straight up, stopping when your left hand has reached the bottom stopper. You can return to attention by sliding the pole back down and grabbing in the center of the silk with your left. Most color guards will practice going from attention to right shoulder and back again over and over until they don't even have to think about the movement.

*In the front present angle, the right arm is completely
extended and the silk is presented forward from the body.*

After a bit of practice, all of these positions will
form a solid base of technique to work from. Check your
positions constantly since it's more difficult to break
a bad habit than to learn a good one. Standing up tall
and raising your chin will make you look poised and
confident, even if at first you don't feel that way.

Let's Go Team Technique Tip: If you are having trouble making sure your flagpole is straight, squeeze as hard as you can with both hands. With both sets of muscles working hard, your flag should right itself.

PRESENTS

Presents are a series of angles that help teach proper placement. When moving into more advanced flag work, you often have to pass through these positions, so it's necessary to make sure they're correct. There are four presents: front, left, right, and back.

From right shoulder, your top hand (right) moves out to the front until your arm is completely extended. Your left hand is still right in front of your belly button since it doesn't move at all. Don't lean forward. When the position is achieved, your silk is presented forward to the audience.

Like a front present, only the top hand moves for a left present. But instead of moving the flag forward, you move from right shoulder to left, until your arm is extended completely and presents the silk to your left. Your right bicep should be in front of your neck. To do a right present, just angle the flag from right shoulder to the right until the flag pole is in front of your right shoulder.

For a back present, the bottom (left) hand moves from right shoulder and the top stays still. Move your left hand out until your left arm is extended and parallel to the ground. This angle is very important, so double-check your position. Is your arm completely extended and flat to the ground? If your left hand is at eye-level, you're up too high. Don't let your top hand come down either. You shouldn't be able to touch the top of your head with your right hand.

SPINS

The most important thing to remember about spins is that they take practice. No one can pick up a flag and instantly do a hundred perfect drop spins. Don't get frustrated if it seems difficult in the beginning.

There are several different types of spins that vary in speed and difficulty. However, they all build off one fundamental spin: the **drop spin** (also known as a push spin). Despite the name, you don't actually drop the flag. The name comes from the way you spin, "dropping" the flag into your left hand as you go. This is a slow spin; the flag makes one complete revolution every two counts.

To perform a drop spin, start at the right shoulder. Let go with your left hand and rotate the flag counter-clockwise with your right, rotating until the pole is straight up and the flag is down. As you are rotating the flag, bring your right down to your waist. Once the flag is straight upside-down, re-grab with your left. How you grab the pole is very important. Your left hand should be thumb down, palm facing away from you. It is essential that you grab the pole below your right hand. If you do this right, your hands will be together, both palms facing away from you, thumbs down. Your left hand must be under your right. That's count one of the spin; you're halfway there.

During count one of a drop spin, your arms should be positioned like this, with the flag pointed upside-down and perpendicular to the ground.

From this position, let go with your right hand. Continue to rotate the flag in a counter-clockwise direction until it completes the spin. Once it's straight up and down, grab again with your right hand, grabbing under your left hand. Doing any kind of spin, you always grab under. Make sure you grab with your thumb up, just like your left. Your hands should be together. That's count two. You've completed a single drop spin. Count three is the same as count one; continue the direction of the spin until the flag is upside-down, and grab under your right hand with your left. Don't forget that your left hand has to be thumb-down and palm away or you can't continue the spin. Count four is the same as count two, and so on.

Always spin at your waist, not at chest or head level, or your arms will tire much quicker and you'll be making it more difficult. Bring your arms down and fight the urge to spin up high. This is a tough habit to break, so don't fall into it.

Let's Go Team Technique Tip: Is your silk rolling up on the pole as you spin? This is a common problem for beginning spinners. Watch your hands and make sure you're not twisting your wrists. With practice and proper placement, this problem will go away.

BALLET AND COLOR GUARD

Often color guards will spend hours working on ballet technique. Since so much of guard work is graceful and controlled, ballet is an excellent skill to have at your disposal. When moving from one position to another on the field, color guards move with their toes pointed and pass through a position called *coupé*. This is where the heel of one foot touches the anklebone of the other. This automatically lifts the chest up and keeps the toes pointed. Like ballet dancers, guards also "spot" their turns. To do this, pick a spot off in the distance and keep your eyes focused on it as you turn. When you reach the point where you can't watch the spot any longer, turn your head quickly around and find that spot again. Not only does this make you look more impressive, it also keeps you from getting dizzy.

Another thing to think about while spinning is watching the pole and not the silk. Depending on wind, silks can look different from person to person, so watch the metal part instead of the fabric. Say out loud, "Down, up! Down, up!" with the spins. You'll always be down on the odd numbers and up on the even. Make sure you're straight up and down on every count; don't under-rotate or over-rotate your spins.

Check to make sure you are spinning flat to the front. Your flag should create a circle in front of you, not off to one side. If you're having problems, try standing a foot away from a wall, facing it. Spin a few drop spins. If you hit the wall with your flag, or come close, you aren't flat to the front. Go slow and check your hands. After you correct yourself, move closer to the wall. Perfect drop spins can be done a few inches from a wall.

As you work on spins, remember to pay attention to the rest of your body. Watch your posture and where you're placing your feet. It may sound strange, but don't bob your head up and down as you spin. While saying "Down, up!" out loud, a lot of people tend to bob their head down and up as well. This is a hard habit to break so make sure you keep your eyes pointed above the horizon. Don't watch your hands once you've got the spin down because this makes you look bored, or worse, unsure of yourself.

You may become frustrated at first while you learn the correct way to spin a flag, but stick with it. Once you've got the technique mastered, you're ready to move on to more advanced flag work.

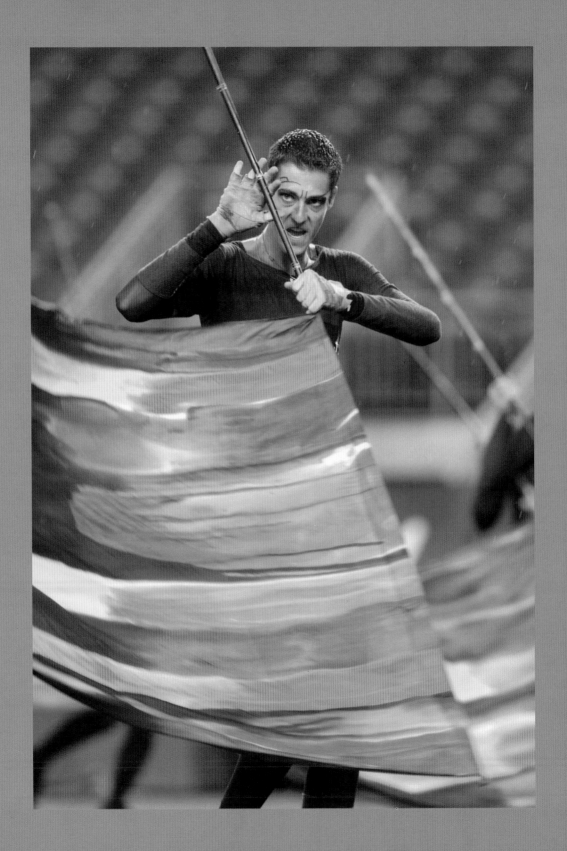

3

Continuing
Technique

This chapter covers some of the more common flag moves used today. It's important to be comfortable with the basic techniques before attempting these more difficult moves. Keep in mind that the names for specific moves vary from guard to guard.

SPIN VARIATIONS

Double-fast spins, sometimes called double-time spins, are a variation of the drop spin. As the name suggests, double-fasts spin twice as fast as a regular drop spin, and are great for warm-up since they give the hands and wrists a workout.

More advanced color guard moves include double-fast spins, peggy spins, and tosses.

The first count of a double-fast spin is the same as the first count of a drop spin. The flag leaves right shoulder and moves upside down, where the left grabs under the right hand, both palms facing away. Count two is where the variation comes in. Continue the spin like a drop spin, but keep rotating the flag past vertical until it is flat. The flag should be parallel to the ground with the silk on the left. Your left hand should be palm up to the sky. Grasp the pole with your right hand the same as your left, palm up. Your hands should be by each other, pinkie fingers touching. That is count two. Practice moving from count one to two several times and get used to the feel of it.

GUARD ORGANIZATIONS

Winter Guard International (WGI) and Drum Corps International (DCI) offer unique competitive opportunities for young people with an interest in guard.

Founded in 1977, Winter Guard International oversees color guard activity, creates standard rules for competition, and provides leadership and guidance to guards. WGI hosts regional contests in the United States, Canada, and Europe, as well as a World Championship. WGI offers competitions at all levels, from beginner to advanced programs and performers.

Founded in 1972, Drum Corps International is a nonprofit youth organization that promotes drum and bugle corps and their color guards. DCI establishes the rules and regulations for drum corps, and it develops educational programs for both drum corps participants and judges. Open to ages 14 to 22, DCI competitions include regional, national, and international contests.

From count two, keep the spin going (rotating counter-clockwise) and drop the flag into your left hand like a drop spin. Your left hand grabs under your right, palms away. Your silk will be up. Count four is just like count two. Rotate the flag up to vertical and continue until it's flat. Grasp it with your right, pinkies together. The flag will be on your right now. Those four counts, repeated over and over again, are double-fast spins.

Peggy spins are similar to double-fasts, but on counts three, five, and seven you break the cardinal rule of spinning and grab above your right hand. Like double-fasts, count one is a drop spin. Count two is also a drop spin, except your right hand grabs the flag differently, in a "hitch." Like a hitchhiker, you stick out your thumb, but your hand is open and palm up to the sky. The pole goes right in the center of the "L" your thumb and index finger form, what some people call the "thumb pit."

From the hitch on count two, rotate the flag in your right hand one full spin until your right hand is thumb-down. That full rotation is excellent for strengthening your wrists, but it can be difficult to control. Squeeze hard with your fingers and don't let the flag control you. After you've rotated the flag a full circle, grasp above your right hand with your palm away. (Just like a drop spin, but with your left hand on top, not the right.) To get to count four, rotate the flag a half circle until the silk is down, and grab it at the hitch. The spin then repeats itself, always grabbing up on the odd numbered counts.

The peggy spin is confusing to someone who is learning double-fast, so it should be taught only after double-fast technique has been mastered. It is important to note that the flag rotates a full spin on odd numbers and only a half spin on even numbers. Basically, the spin looks choppy in comparison to regular double-fasts, which are smooth. Some guards choose to use peggy spins over regular double-fasts to emphasize that their music is not flowing or continuous.

THE PREP

The **prep** is a four-count spin that prepares the flag for a toss. Starting from right shoulder, do three counts of double-fast spins. At count three the flag is straight up and down with the silk right-side up. The left hand is below the right and both hands are palms away, thumbs down. To get to count four, rotate the flag less than you normally would for a regular double-fast spin (counter-clockwise), until it is at a 45-degree angle from the ground, silk down. As you rotate the flag to this angle, grab halfway into the silk with your right hand, palm up. Do not grab with your palm down because you can't toss from this position.

Counts one through four are continuous. Don't pause on any count. However, these four counts do have set positions, which means you can't just slop through them. Count four has to be at an angle, not flat or vertical. This angle will help you when it comes time to release the flag.

THE TOSS

The standard **toss** can be done without any prep, but it's helpful to have a nice clean spin before the release.

Not only does it prepare you for the toss, it is more visually stunning this way.

From the angle at count four, push down with your left hand and let go while lifting up with your right. Don't let go of the flag with your right hand, let the end swing up toward the sky. Stop the flag when it is at an opposite 45-degree angle. Your right hand should be up as if for a high five. When you actually toss the flag, release at this point—when the flag has rotated enough and has enough lift to get up in the air. Set back up at the angle at count four and try that move a few times without releasing. Both arms have to work together. The left hand pulls down on the flag while the right lifts up.

Now you're ready to actually let go of the flag. Remember, you can't let go of the pole with your right hand until it's up above your head or it won't go up in the air. If the flag spins in front of you quickly and hits the ground, you're releasing too soon. If it goes up in the air, but doesn't rotate, you're probably not pulling down with your left hand. Strength doesn't really play much part in tossing. It's all in the timing. Make sure both arms are working to get the flag up and around.

Try a couple releases without worrying about catching them. Don't be afraid of the flag; you control it and it only does what you tell it to. After you try a few, try to catch one after it has done one and a half rotations, so the flag is straight up and down with the silk on top. Your hands should catch it in the attention position. When you catch, the flag should have rotated enough so that both hands grab the pole at the same time.

Proper timing is the key to a successful toss. If you are practicing indoors, make sure the ceilings are high enough to allow you to toss the flag without hitting the ceiling.

Like drop spins, tossing doesn't come easily. Expect a few hours of dropping the flag more than catching it. If you practice, before you know it you'll be snatching that flag out of the sky in a perfect catch.

Keep your feet planted firmly on the ground. Everyone goes up on their toes when they release at first, but try not to. Going up on your toes is a natural instinct, but it actually causes you to toss the flag lower. Pretend someone has glued your feet, particularly your heels, to the floor. Have a friend or parent watch your feet while you practice a few tosses. You may be surprised to learn that you were going up on your toes when you didn't think you were.

Check out your free hands while the flag is spinning in the air. Your left hand should hang by the side of your body. Your right hand should be up in the air, ready for that imaginary high five. Like a Barbie doll, your fingers should be together, but your thumb should be detached, waiting to catch the pole. Don't let your arm hang like a dead stick. You want everything about the toss to be impressive. Weak arms can make even the best toss look bad.

After you have perfected your release and catch, try a few tosses with the prep. Make sure you don't pause on count five. The flag should spin at your waist for four counts and then suddenly appear to leap up into the air. If you pause, it will break this effect. When tossing with the prep, make sure that you are still grabbing down halfway into the silk. The prep shouldn't actually affect the toss or the power you put behind it. When tossing outside, don't forget to pay attention to which way the wind is blowing. Adjust your release point to compensate, especially if it's fairly windy.

Let's Go Team Technique Tip: Use vinyl tape to cover your top stopper. This will help the silk slide off instead of getting caught in an unattractive sail.

AROUND THE WORLD

An **around the world** is a fairly common move, but it takes a full eight counts to complete. It's called an around the world because it starts at right shoulder and ends

When tossing, always keep both feet firmly on the ground. Going up on your toes will cause your tosses to be lower.

there, but it goes all the way around you. As with most moves, remember your checkpoints.

Starting at right shoulder, sweep the flag down toward the ground (counter-clockwise), tucking the pole part of the flag under your right arm. On count one, the flag is down at an angle and the pole is under your arm. To get to count two, continue the sweep past your toes and bring the flag up. As you raise your right arm, bring up your left, too. At count two your arms are raised up at 45-degree angles, in a high "V."

Count three is a bit tricky. This is where you execute a move known as a **backscratcher.** Just like it sounds, you use the flag to scratch your back. Not literally, of course, but you have to rotate the flag in your right hand until the tip of the pole is in the center of your back. The pole is straight up and down, silk part down behind your back. Grab with your left hand just above your right hand, with your thumb down. This position is count three. From here, open up your arms, letting go with your right hand. The flag will come up and your arms will again be in that high V, but this time the flag is in your left hand. So count two and four are the same, except the flag is on opposite sides of your body.

Those four counts should be practiced several times until you get the motion down. The flag moves in one continuous motion without any direction changes. Remember the checkpoints and keep your circles flat to the front. Like drop spins, you should be able to do an around the world only a few inches from a wall. You can also say "Down, up! Down, up!" during these counts since the flag does exactly that.

From count four, lower your arms and let the pole tuck under your left arm. Count five is at an angle pointing away from your toes. Now bring the flag straight up and down. Hitch your right hand under your left. Remember,

In order to complete an around the world, you have to do a move known as the "backscratcher" for the way it looks when the tip of the flagpole is pointed down behind your back.

at the hitch your hand is flat and palm up. This is count six. For count seven, let go with the left hand and rotate the flag until it is set in the hitch. Close your fingers around the pole, continuing to turn the flag until it's straight upside-down. This is the checkpoint for count seven. Continue to rotate the pole until you bring it back up to right shoulder, leaving your top hand inverted.

SIDESPINS

After an around the world, you can move directly into **sidespins.** As implied by the name, the flag spins on your side. From right shoulder, invert your top hand (if you just finished an around the world, your hand is already switched). Push the flag out forward and let go with your left hand. Sweep the flag on the left side of your body, letting the pole part of the flag cross over onto the right side of you. Like drop spins, it's down on count one and up on count two. Continue the side spin on the right side of your body, as if the silk of the flag is chasing the other end of the pole. After being down on count three and up on four, repeat counts one and two for five and six. However, at count six grab the flag with your left hand on top, thumb up. Then do a drop spin on seven, continuing up to right shoulder on eight.

Let's Go Team Technique Tip: With all of these moves, remember to stay either completely flat to the front or to the side. Visualization can help. Imagine yourself in a giant toaster slot. If you don't keep your flag straight up and down you're going to get stuck inside the toaster.

Routines and Movement

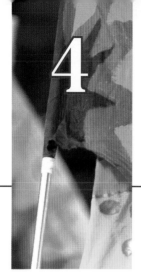

Now that you've mastered several different moves, you're ready to start putting them together in succession. This is known as choreography. For something simple such as a warm-up or a tryout routine, you probably don't need to worry about music. You can just come up with several eight counts and put them together in a series. Like dance, color guard routines are typically measured in eights. For a more advanced routine, you can set your flag work to music. It's important to understand a little bit about music before doing this, though.

Music is divided into measures. How many beats (counts) a measure has, depends on the time signature.

In addition to flags, rifles, and sabers, color guard routines also involve dance and movement, and guard members use their body language to enhance their performance.

The majority of music is in 4/4 time. This means each measure has four counts. Another common time signature is 3/4. This means every measure has three counts. With a time signature of 3/4, usually you count in sixes instead of eights. If you're counting in eights and a song has 100 measures, you'll need choreography for 50 eights.

To give you a rough estimate, the song "Drops of Jupiter" as recorded by the band Train, is 4:17 long, and has about 42 eights, since it is 83 measures long.

Let's Go Team Technique Tip: Music can change time signatures in the middle of a song, or even just for a couple measures. This can make for some tricky counting.

When choosing music, remember to think about your audience. Try to pick music that appeals to everyone, especially people of different ages. No matter how good your routine is, if your audience can't stand the music, they probably won't enjoy the performance. The song should allow you to express yourself, and the flag work and movement should complement the song.

Keep your mind open to several different types of music. Perhaps you don't like jazz in general, but if someone suggests a song to you, give it a listen. You might find the lyrics or beat appealing. Music gives you many different options and lets you show off your creativity and originality.

If you're having a tough time deciding, consider your strengths. Are you graceful and do you like flowing flag moves? Then you're going to want to stick with a slower song. If you are better at hard flag moves and quick direction changes, opt for something more up-tempo.

Don't forget that a routine is more than just spinning a flag. It involves movement and dance as well. Try to choose a song that has variety or is musically interesting. Some color guards won't even consider a song unless it has a definite mood change in it. This shows off both sides of the guard, slow and fast.

Once you've chosen your song, you're ready to start choreographing. Take out a sheet of lined paper and listen carefully to the music. As the song starts, write down an eight in the margin on each line, counting as you go through the song. This will let you know how many eights you need to choreograph. Perhaps you already have a few ideas in mind for a certain section of the song. Listen to it again, still counting along, but this time make notes beside the eights that are special. For example, if there is a part in the music that a toss would accentuate, circle that eight. Draw brackets around the chorus/refrain of a song, in case you want to repeat moves.

Don't forget dance when you're writing a routine. Every single count doesn't have to be filled with flag movement. Let the music guide you here. Don't just start dancing because you've run out of ideas. Does your style reflect the song? Make sure you're not doing graceful ballet-type moves to a fast song, or hip hop to a slow love song.

For inspiration, try watching music videos. The artists put energy behind each move, even if it's just a simple head turn. When you write your routine, remember to give yourself room to sell it; you want to write interesting moves that you can really perform. Musicals are good to watch, too. Like the characters in the cheerleading movie *Bring It On,* keep your mind open to all different types of performing arts. You never know what type of inspiration you might get.

STRETCHES

Start off with some stretches, especially the wrists, whenever putting in some serious flag time. Put your hands together, as when praying, then try to push your elbows up towards your fingertips. Stretch to the point of tightness, not pain. From this position, turn your hands upside down, so that the underside of your wrists is pointing up to the sky.

Repeat these two stretches, but this time, put the backs of your hands together. Notice how the stretch feels

THE JAZZ RUN

A special marching technique that is particular to color guard is a controlled run called the jazz run. The jazz run is often used for staging purposes, when the color guard must move quickly to a new location on the field. Rather than jogging, color guards use the jazz run to keep their upper bodies still while their feet move in step to the tempo. Since the upper body doesn't move, the arms remain at the sides instead of swinging like a runner's would. When jazz running, remember to keep your toes pointed and your feet as close to the ground as possible. Don't pick up your legs and always lead with your toes. When jazz running is properly executed, it should look controlled, graceful, and effortless.

different? After you've completed those stretches, ball your hands into fists and roll your wrists a few times. Some people also use this stretch: grab your fingertips with the other hand and push the heel of your palm away from you for a few seconds, then turn your wrist upside-down for the opposite stretch. Repeat for the other hand. After you've stretched your wrists out, warm up the rest of your body with some arm circles and shoulder rolls.

Extend your arm across your body and pull it toward you for a few seconds. Release your arm, extend it up, and bend it back behind you, like you're patting yourself on the back. Grab that elbow and pull it gently behind your head. Repeat both of these with the other arm. Don't forget to breathe through all your stretches; never hold your breath.

WARM-UP ROUTINE

Warm-up routines actually have many other functions besides warming the muscles. They can teach tempo, good placement, and concentration, and they can calm nerves before a big performance. When writing a warm-up routine, remember to warm up both sides of the body equally. Variety is important to keep everyone thinking as they are spinning.

Start out at right shoulder, making sure you have a good clean starting position. From here you can go right into drop spins or a flat exercise. For example, one high school guard says, "Eyes, waist, eyes, up!" during a flat exercise. Their flag does just that, going to flat at the eyes, the waist, back to the eyes, and then returning to right

A color guard performs in unison at a 2002 Drum Corps International competition. Good choreography matches the right movements to the music that is being played.

shoulder. Then they rotate their upper body 90 degrees, and repeat the exercise on one side of their body. The third time they do it again, facing the front, and lastly on the other side of their body.

Start out moving every four counts. At right shoulder, move the flag flat in front of your eyes on count one, holding counts two through four. Then bring the flag down until it's at waist level on count five, holding six through eight. Keep moving every four counts, but remember to keep the movement crisp. Just because there isn't any flag work on counts two, three, and four doesn't mean you're not performing. The rests are as important as the moves. After you go through the routine once in fours, try it in twos, moving every other count. After completing the twos, do the routine once through without any pauses. That's a great warm-up and makes for clean flats.

Another good warm-up is 100 counts of drop-spins, 100 to the left and 100 to the right. This is very tiring at first, but before long you'll be doing 300 spins without difficulty. As you spin in a group, everyone should shout out the tens. This keeps everyone counting together. On the last ten, everyone should count every count out loud, so they will all stop together. If done correctly, it'll be something like this: "Eighty! Ninety! One, two, three, four, five, six, seven, eight, nine, one hundred!"

DRILL

Drill is a chart or image that tells the color guard exactly where they should be on the floor or field at any given time in the music. The music is divided into **sets,** or different color guard formations. It's important to realize that there is no standard number of sets since it depends on the song you've chosen and how many people you have.

To read drill, first figure out what interval it's been written in. Depending on how the drill was written, the intervals can vary greatly. Some drill writing programs just go off the yard lines and hash marks drawn on a football field. Others break down each individual step on the field with a grid. When looking at a football field, everything to the left of the 50 yard line is considered Side I. Side II is to the right of the 50 yard line. If you are directly in between two yard lines, such as the 35 and 40 on Side I, you're "splitting" these two yard lines. If you're one step closer to the 40, you're three steps outside the 40. If you're one step closer to 35, you're three steps inside the 35. Going toward the 50 is always inside, regardless of the side you're on.

In high school, the front and back hash marks are three eights plus four steps from the sideline. In college, they are four eights. Most fields have only one set of hashes, so make sure you know which hash mark you're looking at.

Depending on a show, you might have 50 or 60 sets. You may find it helpful to create a coordinate book instead of lugging around tons of charts. A coordinate book is just a small note pad that has your individual coordinates for each set. For example, it might say something like "Side II, one step inside the 35, 11 steps up from the back hash," for high school hashes.

Some instructors require you to have your drill charts with you at all times. You've most likely been assigned a number, so go through each set and highlight your number. Some people like to highlight the entire color guard line in one color and their individual number in a different color so they can see the whole formation. It's best then to buy a sturdy binder and clear plastic sheet protectors. You'll need one for every two sets of drill.

Let's Go Team Technique Tip: Plastic sheet protectors can open different ways; the ones where the opening is closest to the rings of the binder is the best. This way you can hold your binder at any angle and the charts won't slide out. Plastic protectors keep the drill clean and dry, while allowing you to flip through them easily.

If your drill has not been printed on both sides of the paper, take set one and two and put the backs together, making sure that the pages are facing exactly the way you want them before you slide them into the protectors. Repeat this for all the sets until you're done and you should have a nice book that will stand up to any weather. Don't forget to put your name on it.

MARCHING

Now that you understand where to go, you need to know how to get there. There are several different types of marching styles, but we'll cover only the two most common: **roll step** (also called glide step) and **chair step** (also called high step). Most high schools and drum corps use roll step. Half the university and college marching bands use chair step.

As with all forms of marching, you always begin and end with the left foot. When you step off (move forward) it is always with your left, even if you're heading to the right or going backwards.

For roll step, when moving forward you "roll" your foot. As you step, place the end of your heel on the ground and then roll through the bottom of your foot until you get to your toes. As your toes get to the ground, you're already picking up your heel. Likewise, when your heel is down, your toes need to be up, pointing towards the sky. This is why you hear instructors yell, "Toes up!" when a marching band is practicing. The result is a smooth motion; you "glide" across the field while keeping your upper body straight.

Regardless of which direction your feet are heading, keep your upper body toward the front. Make sure your shoulders are parallel to the front sideline. As you spin your flag, keep it flat to the front at all times. Flag work looks different from behind; if half the color guard was spinning facing back and the other was forward, half the silks would be going the wrong way.

When moving backwards, instead of rolling your feet, you go up on your toes. From the moment you step off to the moment you reach your mark, you must stay up on the balls of your feet. Try to stand as tall as you can. Just getting air under your heels isn't enough. Extend your legs as hard as possible and think about how great your calf muscles will look in a few weeks.

Marking time is the term used to describe marching in place. You're keeping the tempo, but not moving in any direction. Stand in third position and pretend the balls of your feet have been glued to the ground. You can still lift your heels, but can't lift your whole foot. Your heels move to the tempo, heels hitting the ground on the beat. Remember to start and end with the left foot. Odd counts are always the left, even counts are the right foot.

When learning proper roll step, practice a few **eight to five** drills. Eight to five is a shortened phrase used in place of eight steps for every five yards. If someone says, "A four to five step," that means four steps for every five yards, or every yard line, since yard lines are five yards apart. Most instructors spend a lot of time teaching eight to five. As you're doing drills, remember that you need to take eight steps to reach the next yard line, which means you need to be halfway (but no more) by count four. Take all eight counts to get there, but not with huge steps for six counts, then two baby steps. Equal size steps the whole way will make your drills a lot easier.

If you can't practice on a field, use two books to mark off the five-yard distance between two yard lines in your backyard or in a park. Try a drill that is called **eights & eights.** It goes like this: eight counts of mark time, eight counts forward; eight counts mark time, eight counts back. Repeat four times. Work on keeping your toes up as you march forward, and staying up on the balls of your feet as you march backwards.

Put on some music that's upbeat as you try this exercise. Remember to keep time with the music, stepping off on count one with your left foot. As you move forward, plant your right foot on the yard line on count eight, then bring in your left foot to close the "T" your feet make on the second count one. If it helps, count out loud for the first seven counts, then say, "Turn out, close!" instead of counts eight and one. Also, when marching backwards, don't come back down onto your heels until count one.

When doing drills, always hit the yard line with your heel, never the arch of your foot or toes. If some people hit the yard line with something other than their heel, it throws off lines. As you become more comfortable with this marching style, don't watch your feet. Pick out a spot far away above the horizon and focus your eyes on that instead. This pulls your chin up and makes you look impressive and confident. Use your peripheral vision (what you see out of the corners of your eyes) to make sure you're still hitting the yard lines correctly.

Chair step is a bit more complicated and strenuous than roll step. Stand up straight and lift your left leg up until your thigh is parallel to the ground and let your leg dangle straight down. Point your toes toward the ground and you have a perfect chair position. As you mark time in this position, each leg has to come up until the thigh is parallel to the ground. Push your feet out and up off the ground, but don't kick out. Your toes should always be in a straight line with your knee.

Stand near a wall as you practice marking time. Try to lightly tap your shoe laces against the wall as you mark time. Keep your abdominal muscles in tight and use them to help pull your legs up into that chair position. Not only is it tiring, it's also very difficult to keep this step clean. As you're practicing, you might be wondering how you're going to be able to spin a flag with your feet out in front of you. When marching chair style, you hold the flag a few extra inches away from your body to allow for this.

When moving, trace a line across the ground with your toes. As your right toes pass your left ankle you can start to bring up your leg. Don't bring that knee up until your toes have passed the ankle or you get an effect called bicycling. This is where you bring the knee up too soon and look like you're pedaling a bicycle. Start at a slow tempo and bring that knee up at the right time.

Unlike roll step, you always march forward in chair style. To reverse direction, simply turn and head back in the opposite direction.

The two most common marching styles are roll step, also known as glide step, and chair step, also called high step.

Don't let your upper body bounce or move as you march. You might need to lower your center an inch or two to help keep you still. Remember, your legs need to be independent of your upper body—there should be no movement in your shoulders when you are marking time.

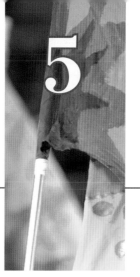

Joining a Guard

If you decide to try out for a color guard or winter guard, chances are you're going to have to go through an audition. Mostly these auditions aren't about what you can and cannot do, but how hard you're willing to practice. Auditions usually take two or three days to complete—one or two to learn a routine and the third to perform for a panel of judges. If you don't receive a written copy of the routine, try to write one out yourself, and have one of the instructors check it to make sure it's correct. Bring a blank tape with you so that you can get a copy of the music. This will help tremendously when practicing.

When auditioning for a guard, you will be given time to practice learning a routine before performing it for the judges.

Even if you don't feel like you're doing well when learning the routine, remember that you have time to practice. Most judges just want to see improvement from when you first learned the routine. This shows them that you have been working on your own.

Prepare for an interview. Sometimes instructors will want to see what your personality is like before they take you into their group. They might ask you questions like, "Why do you want to be in this group?" Try to think of some answers ahead of time so you can really wow them with a thoughtful answer. Be yourself and smile. Color guard can be a lot of fun, so make sure you look like you're enjoying yourself. Before and after the audition, walk with your head held high and look confident. If you get nervous, take a deep breath and smile.

Let's Go Team Technique Tip: Look presentable during your audition; also make sure you wear an outfit that is comfortable enough for the routine.

FORM, BODY, AND EQUIPMENT

In color guard, form, body, and equipment form a triad of important things to remember. You need to concentrate on these three elements. Your form is where you belong within the group. You should always be checking to make sure your spacing is correct. Even when you are spinning equipment, you still need to watch your body, especially your upper body and free hand. Lastly, you need to make sure you are executing all the moves with the equipment correctly and at the right time.

Like color guard, winter guard uses flags and other props, but it is performed indoors instead of on a field or in a parade. Many guard members participate in both color and winter guard.

Color guard is "the sport of the arts," bringing beauty and precision to an audience. It is an exciting activity for both men and women that combines hard work, dedication, and skill. Since its beginning, color guard has been rapidly growing throughout North America. By following the techniques described in this book, you will have a solid base of skills to work from, and be ready to move into the more advanced flag work that colleges and winter guards have now made the standard.

Glossary

around the world – An eight-count move that begins and ends with right shoulder and goes all the way around the body.

attention – A specific position where a color guard member stands motionless.

backscratcher – A move in which the flag is rotated until the tip of the pole is aligned with the center of the guard's back (it looks like the guard member is scratching her back with the flagpole).

chair step – A step where the marcher's leg is raised and forms a position like a chair.

choreography – The linking of moves together in a specific succession.

coupé – A ballet position in which the heel of one foot touches the anklebone of the other.

double-fast spin – Spins that rotate twice as fast as drop spins.

double-time spin – Another name for a double-fast spin.

drill – A chart that shows exact placement on the field or floor.

drop spin – A basic spin that rotates once every two counts.

eights & eights – A drill in which guards do eight counts of mark time followed by eight counts of forward marching, then eight counts of mark time followed by eight counts of backward marching.

eight to five drill – A common color guard drill in which guards take eight steps to cover five yards on the field.

flat – A position where the flagpole is parallel to the ground.

hash marks – Small lines drawn parallel to the sidelines on a football field. Marchers use these lines to assist them in their placement.

hitch – A hand position in which the thumb is stuck out.

mark time – Term for when a marcher keeps the beat and marches in place.

peggy spin – A variation of the double-fast spin where the flag is grabbed up on every other count.

prep – A four-count spin that prepares the flag for a toss.

present – An angle that the flag makes in a specific direction.

push spin – Another name for a drop spin.

ready – Another term for the attention position.

right shoulder – A position where the right hand is at the tape and the left hand is at the bottom stopper and by the waist.

roll step – A step where the bottom of the foot is rolled along the ground.

set – A specific formation that a group makes.

side spins – One-handed spins that are done on either side of the body.

slam – An angle that the flag makes when one hand is at the tape and the other at the bottom stopper.

third position – A ballet position where the feet are turned out to form a "T."

thumb pit – Term for the center of the L-shaped space between the thumb and index finger.

toss – A move where the pole leaves the hands and rotates in the air.

Internet Resources

http://www.angelfire.com/band/truecolors
> The author's own color guard Web site, offering information and links related to high school guards and college guards, as well as basic technique information and links to color guard suppliers.

http://www.bands.org
> The Bands of America (BOA) Web site provides information on BOA events, which attract over 60,000 students each year.

http://www.dci.org/corps
> Drum Corps International (DCI) sponsors worldwide competition for drum and bugle corps.

http://www.marchinglinks.com
> Marchinglinks.com is a comprehensive site for marching band and the performance arts, listing resources for color guard, drum corps, and marching band, including classifieds, uniform and equipment suppliers, designers, circuits, events, and publications.

http://www.tob.org
> The Tournament of Bands (TOB) is a competitive band organization open to any middle school, high school, college, or university band in the United States.

http://www.wamsb.org
> The World Association of Marching Show Bands (WAMSB) is an international group dedicated to promoting global communication and interaction between marching show bands and encouraging participation in marching show bands.

http://www.wgi.org
> Winter Guard International (WGI) sponsors regional marching band competitions as well as U.S. and Canadian contests for color and winter guard.

Further Reading

Bailey, Wayne, and Thomas Caneva. *The Complete Marching Band Resource Manual.* Philadelphia: University of Pennsylvania Press, 1994.

Garty, Judy. *Marching Band Competition.* Philadelphia: Mason Crest Publishers, 2003.

Garty, Judy. *Techniques of Marching Bands.* Philadelphia: Mason Crest Publishers, 2003.

Usilton, Terry. *Color Guard Competition.* Philadelphia: Mason Crest Publishers, 2003.

Valliant, Doris. *Going to College* (Let's Go Team: Cheer, Dance, March). Philadelphia: Mason Crest Publishers, 2003.

Vickers, Steve. *A History of Drum and Bugle Corps.* Madison, Wisconsin: Sights and Sounds, Inc., 2002.

Index

KARYN SLOAN is a two-time Indiana State Champion, a Bands of America Regional Champion and National Finalist, and she has competed in over thirty competitions. In 1998 she received the Outstanding Flag Corps Member Award from Purdue's "All-American" Marching Band, where she was captain during the 1999–2000 season. She has taught color guard at several high schools and is currently the Color Guard Director for Marshall High School in Marshall, Wisconsin.